MILLIE MERMAID WANTS TO GO TO SCHOOL

A 'Let's Talk About It' Book

MISS SANDY'S
SEASIDE SCHOOL
WHERE SCHOOLING IS COOL

written by
Janet McCormick

AuthorHouse™
1663 Liberty Drive
Bloomington, IN 47403
www.authorhouse.com
Phone: 833-262-8899

Because of the dynamic nature of the Internet, any web addresses or links contained in this book may have changed since publication and may no longer be valid. The views expressed in this work are solely those of the author and do not necessarily reflect the views of the publisher, and the publisher hereby disclaims any responsibility for them.

This book is printed on acid-free paper.

ISBN: 979-8-8230-1225-6 (sc)
ISBN: 979-8-8230-1226-3 (e)

Library of Congress Control Number: 2023913832

Print information available on the last page.

Published by AuthorHouse 08/01/2023

authorHOUSE®

What is a
'Let's Talk About It' book?

The approach in *Millie Mermaid Wants to Go to School* is more than anything else **interactive.** It gives early learners a meaningful way to participate in the story. While the characters and backgrounds might be unique, the scenarios will be familiar to their own experience—beginning school, having to wait for a big day, making friends, etc. Responding to the questions in the story provides an opportunity to verbalize and share *their* feelings, encounters, and insights. This interactive conversation helps develop a larger vocabulary, gain more self-confidence, and increase their prediction and problem-solving skills.

Suitable for teachers, parents, or caregivers, the suggested questions and comments within the book help reveal the young child's world. The more animated the reader, the more engaged the child(ren) will be. Allowing ample time for answers encourages a dialogue that creates a safe space for sharing, even for those who might be shy and reluctant.

Here are several options for reading:

A) Read and Respond – read the story including questions, giving time for reflection and response.

B) Show and Tell – show each page and ask the child(ren) to make up a story about the picture.

C) A Combination – Use Read and Respond for a portion of the book, then show the remaining pages and ask how they think the story ends.

So, buckle up and enjoy the ride. You never know what you'll learn along the way!

Janet McCormick

MILLIE MERMAID
WANTS TO GO TO SCHOOL

* * * * * *

A 'Let's Talk About It' book

Why Can't I Go to School Too?

Millie wanted to be just like her big sister, Kate. She wanted to do everything that Kate did – swim fast, dive deep down in the ocean, and play mermaid games. She tried hard to keep up, but Kate and her friends thought she was just too slow – at least that's what they told her.

Do you have an older brother or sister?

What are some of the things you've wanted to do?

"Mommy, why doesn't Kate want me to play with her?

Her friends laugh at me and call me names just because I can't swim as fast as they can. That's mean and makes me sad. If I could go to school like Kate does, I'd swim much faster and learn new games. Why can't I go to school too?"

Were you 'just waiting' to go to school – or were you not quite so sure?

Her mom shook her head and said, "I'm sorry, Millie. You're not old enough to go to school like Kate. Besides, school isn't like a play date. There's lots to learn. After your next birthday we'll take you to Miss Sandy's Seaside School and you can see what it's like."

Do you like to wait for a special day?

How do you think Millie felt?

Millie didn't like her mother's answer one bit. That meant she would have to wait, wait, and wait some more. She was tired of waiting to get bigger and do fun things. It made her so sad, she started to cry.

"I don't think I'll ever be old enough to do the things that Kate does. Why does she have all the fun?"

Let's make a sad face.

What could you say to help Millie feel better?

Her mom saw how unhappy Millie was and reached out to give her a big hug.

"I'm sorry Millie. I know it's hard to wait. The next time we go to the store, why don't we look for a special ribbon for your hair for your first day at school?"

That made Millie feel much better!

What are some of the things that make you feel better when you're sad?

Now we can put on our happy face.

On Millie's next birthday her mom set up a visit with Miss Sandy at Seaside School. This is what Millie had been waiting for. She was so excited and asked lots of questions.

Were you happy, excited, or a little worried thinking about starting school?

"There's lots of things here to play with. Do we play all day? What if others don't like me and won't play with me?" Miss Sandy smiled and answered, "Oh, Millie, don't worry. We have lots of games and lessons to help everyone have fun and get along together."

Millie seems a little nervous.

What was something you wanted to do first?

Do you remember something that surprised you about school?

Millie looked puzzled and asked, "What's the difference between games and lessons? Why don't we just play with our new friends?"

Miss Sandy laughed and said, "Lots of others have asked that question. Part of school is doing activities that might look like a game, but you also learn things you'll use later - like how to swim in a line with others or form a circle and count to twenty." Millie giggled. "That sounds like fun! I can't wait to start."

Do you think Millie will like school?

Why?

What advice would you give her?

Notes and Questions

Printed in the United States
by Baker & Taylor Publisher Services